THE SHAKER DAYBOOK

Edited by
David Larkin and June Sprigg

Photographs by
Michael Freeman and Paul Rocheleau

A DAVID LARKIN BOOK

EBURY PRESS STATIONERY

We would like to thank the following institutions:

Hancock Shaker Village
Shakertown at Pleasant Hill, Kentucky
The Western Reserve Historical Society, Cleveland
The United Society of Shakers, Sabbathday Lake, Maine
Canterbury Shaker Village, Inc., Canterbury, New Hampshire
The Shaker Museum and Library, Old Chatham, New York
The Fruitlands Museums, Harvard, Massachusetts

First published in Great Britain by
Ebury Press Stationery
An imprint of the Random Century Group
Random Century House, 20 Vauxhall Bridge Road,
London SW1V 2SA

ISBN 0-09-175151-9

Printed in Italy by Sfera/Garzanti

SFE 10 9 8 7 6 5 4 3 2 1

Introduction

"Do all your work as if you had a thousand years to live on earth, and as you would if you knew you must die tomorrow."
MOTHER ANN LEE (1736–1784)

Those familiar with the Shakers will probably already know how important daybooks and journals were in the daily life of the United Society of Believers, America's longest lived and most influential communal utopian society. We who study that life are endlessly grateful for the thousands of volumes and pages that record the tens of thousands of days that have passed since the Shakers' spiritual mother Ann Lee brought her vision to America from her native England in 1774.

But we must remember that, however useful to us, the daybooks and journals were not written for us, outside the community and further removed by time. The Shakers wrote these volumes for themselves, as a record of events in the life of each communal family, from the humble quotidian—the date of planting peas in the spring, the number of barrels of cider pressed, to the milestones—the death of a beloved leader, the opening of the testimony in the western states of Kentucky and Ohio, the building of a splendid new barn or dwelling.

In writing accounts of their daily experience, the Shakers were cut from the same bolt as their New England neighbors, who were likewise uncommonly given to recording their days in diary form. Literate, thrifty, and driven to relentless productivity by a combination of hilly ground, tough winters, and religious background, many Yankees filled small volumes with a line or two per day, recording in the sparest of autobiographies the pleasures and sorrows of their lives and particularly what they accomplished. For the Shakers, who had been told by Mother Ann, "Put your hands to work and your hearts to God, and a blessing will attend you," the urge to make work the measure of their days was if anything even stronger.

But Shaker diarists differed from their worldly counterparts in a significant way. Worldly diaries were private records of individual lives. Each diarist wrote about self for self. Shaker "scribes," in contrast, were assigned the job of writing about the family for the family. In Shaker life, the singularly solitary and individual task of journalizing was given over to the needs of the community. Shaker journals were not intended to be private, ever, because privacy was suspect in a society which valued union, uniformity, and the good of the group above all. Even the leaders' journals, confidential at times and not to be read by the general membership, were available to other leaders or the Ministry.

One can argue that any words committed to paper invite sharing, even the most private diaries of the most private people in the outside world. Still, the Shakers who wrote clearly knew that their words were for all from the moment the ink dried on the page.

Humans are humans, however, and individual voices peep through, to the delight of those of us who prowl the browned pages for whatever nugget of information we're prospecting at the moment. Here, in the power of words on paper, the most fragile of human substances, the long-gone Shakers live—humorous, pious, petulant, kind, weary, saddened, celebrating—just like us. If we view the Shakers as a strand of matched pearls, as they might have wished to be and to be seen—linked, ordered, uniform, shining, lovely, unrevealing, made smooth, round, perfect and whole by layer upon layer of spiritual and communal experience—then in their journals we hear at times the voice of the individual bit of grit that remained at the heart of each pearl.

It is a pleasure to present some of those voices in the journal entries that dot the pages of this daybook, and also to present the photographs of Paul Rocheleau and Michael Freeman, whose time in Shaker villages has recorded other enduring works by Shaker hands. I am grateful to the Western Reserve Historical Society, Cleveland, Ohio, for permission to publish quoted material from their outstanding collection of Shaker manuscripts.

June Sprigg
Pittsfield, Massachusetts
1992

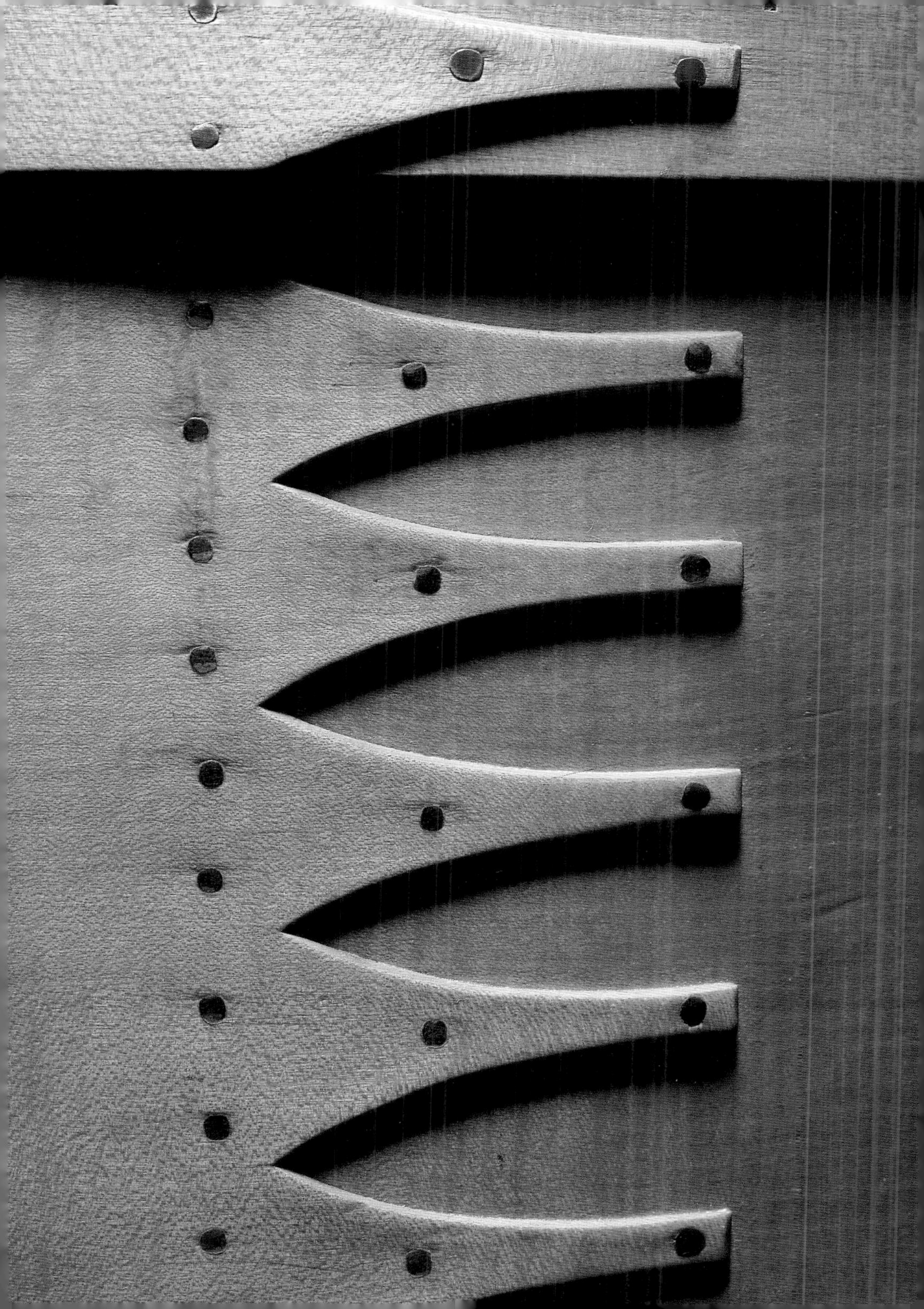

January

1

5

2

6

3

7

4

We'll slick up our rooms
and our halls every one,
Thus the work of the day
is in order begun
And neatness is heaven's adorning.

From a New Year's Covenant
for Sisters under 50 years of age
January 1, 1868

Sister's Shop and Diary, circa 1795-1820

(HANCOCK SHAKER VILLAGE, PITTSFIELD, MASSACHUSETTS)

January

8

12

9

13

10

14

11

Order is my life, my strength and peace.
It paves the way for an endless increase,
Its beauty I love! And keep it I will,
And all gospel graces I will fulfill.
Tho' idols appear to dazzle my eyes,
I will not yield to their vanity and lies.
Peace and good order shall be my aim,
And will be while Luther Wells is my name.

Brother Luther Wells 1858

Round Stone Barn, 1826-64

(HANCOCK SHAKER VILLAGE, PITTSFIELD, MASSACHUSETTS)

January

15

19

16

20

17

21

18

Meetinghouse, 1794

(THE UNITED SOCIETY OF SHAKERS, SABBATHDAY LAKE, MAINE)

During worship, the Shakers pushed the benches out of the way to clear the floor for their distinctive dance.

January

22

23

24

25

26

27

28

Anna Hocknell Departed this life between 4 and 5 o'clock this morning at the Second Order. Anna was the last that was left with us who came from England with our first Parents; she was about 85 years of age.

Brother Philemon Stewart
January 25, 1847

Nurse Shop or Infirmary

(HANCOCK SHAKER VILLAGE, PITTSFIELD, MASSACHUSETTS)

Patients rocked gently to rest in adult cradles.
On the left, the foot of the hospital bed
is raised for comfort.

January/February

29

30

31

1

2

3

4

Case of drawers,
circa 1825-50

(THE SHAKER MUSEUM AND LIBRARY,
OLD CHATHAM, NEW YORK)

February

5

6

7

8

9

10

11

The Sisters are not to comb their heads, wash their feet, smoke, or take snuff, or lay down in any part of the kitchen.

Spirit message from Mother Lucy Wright
February 12, 1839

Cheesemaking in the Sisters' Shop and Dairy, circa 1795-1820

(HANCOCK SHAKER VILLAGE, PITTSFIELD, MASSACHUSETTS)

February

12

16

13

17

14

18

15

Wooden pail, pine, with birch handle
and applewood knob,
shown with pine tub lid.

(CANTERBURY SHAKER VILLAGE, INC.,
CANTERBURY, NEW HAMPSHIRE)

February

19

20

21

22

23

24

25

I am employed in school, school, school,
The same old story.

Brother Giles Avery
February 27, 1832

Detail of yarn reel from Enfield, Connecticut 1825-50

(HANCOCK SHAKER VILLAGE, PITTSFIELD, MASSACHUSETTS)

February/March

26

27

28/29

1

2

3

4

Mother Ann's Birth day The whole Sosiety met in the meeting house, and such a meeting I never saw before. The ministry were there. Elder Joseph spoke first then Elder Brother he said he wanted a free meeting told the young believers that they must not feel straitened, for the meeting was free for all.

Unidentified Brother March 1, 1847
(Mother Ann Lee's birthday on February 29 was customarily celebrated on the day before or after except in Leap Years)

Meetinghouse, 1794

(THE UNITED SOCIETY OF SHAKERS, SABBATHDAY LAKE, MAINE)

Sisters and Brethren entered through separate doors.

March

5

6

7

8

9

10

11

Water House, 1831-33

(SHAKERTOWN AT PLEASANT HILL, HARRODSBURG, KENTUCKY)

Horses powered the pump to fill the 17,600-gallon cistern.

March

12

16

13

17

14

18

15

This is my 47th birthday and my heart is as heavy as lead.

Sister Elizabeth Lovegrove
March 15, 1838

Tailor's tools and Sisters' kerchiefs, circa 1825-50

(HANCOCK SHAKER VILLAGE, PITTSFIELD, MASSACHUSETTS)

March

19

23

20

24

21

25

22

I help build the mill. I presume that there ain't another mill to be found in this state for sawing lumber so copious & snug-built as the aforesaid one.

Brother Elisha Blakeman
March 19, 1836

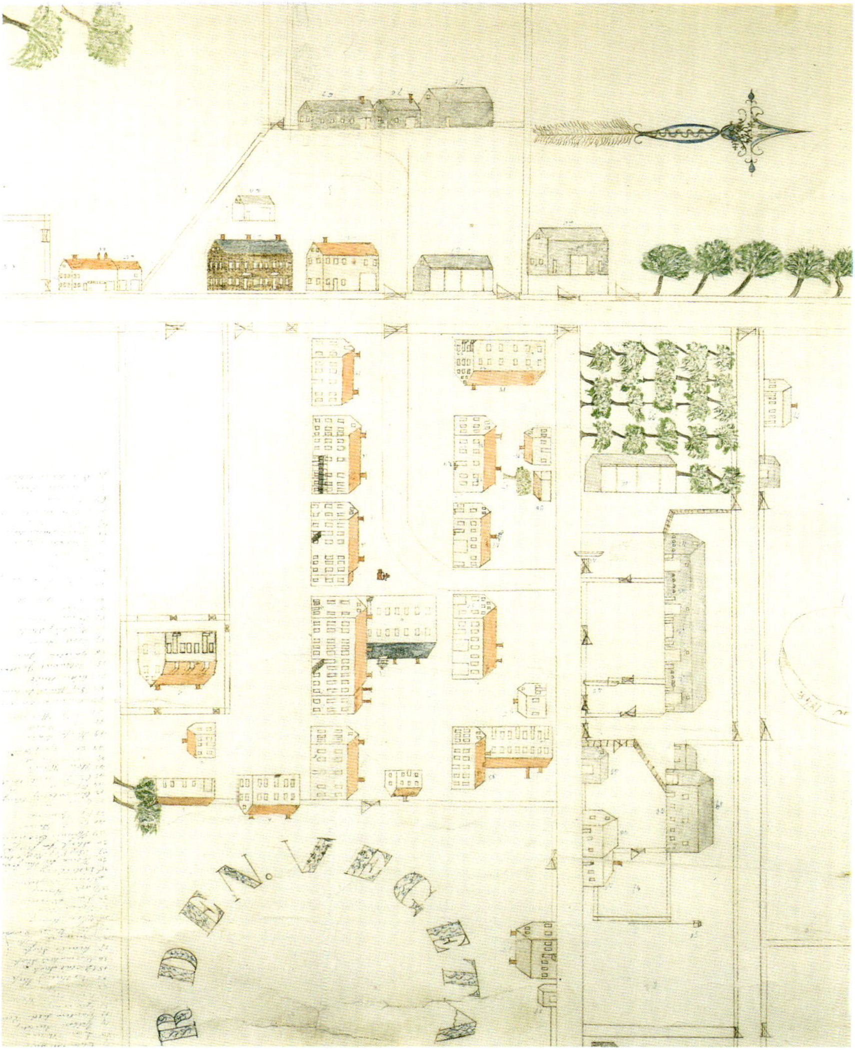

Detail of the Church Family from map of Canterbury Shaker Village, New Hampshire, 1848, by Henry Blinn

(CANTERBURY SHAKER VILLAGE, INC., CANTERBURY, NEW HAMPSHIRE)

The artist drew his communal family's dwelling, office, barns, workshops, and the community's first building, the Meetinghouse, built in 1792.

March/April

26

27

28

29

30

31

1

Case of forty-eight drawers,
originally built-in, circa 1825-50

(HANCOCK SHAKER VILLAGE,
PITTSFIELD, MASSACHUSETTS)

April

2

3

4

5

6

7

8

Oval box,
circa 1845-70

(HANCOCK SHAKER VILLAGE,
PITTSFIELD, MASSACHUSETTS)

April

9

10

11

12

13

14

15

Finish makeing basket's make 800 for sale & 60 odd for home use. The hands have been Prudence Morrel, Eliza Ann Taylor, Elizett Bates, Matilda Reed, Mariah Lapsley, Harriet Goodwin, & Elizabeth Sidle. Daniel Boler prepares their timber for them. He took it when Elder Br John left it; has had it too years.

Sister Betsy Bates April 11, 1835

Apple basket, circa 1835-70

(THE SHAKER MUSEUM AND LIBRARY, OLD CHATHAM, NEW YORK)

April

16

17

18

19

20

21

22

Each one sung what they felt the most gift in, and every song was full of love; David seemed to be devoted to helping the youth, for every time I saw him he had hold of some one or other of them by the hand leading them on to God; Isaac Youngs had little James in his arms with his little hands clinched fast round his neck marching round, he said that he felt very unwell and hardly able to come to meeting when he came, but now he felt like another creature.

Sister Elizabeth Lovegrove April 16, 1827

Meeting Room, Church Family Dwelling, 1830

(HANCOCK SHAKER VILLAGE, PITTSFIELD, MASSACHUSETTS)

The communal family brought their chairs when they gathered here to worship.

April

23

24

25

26

27

28

29

Double desk,
circa 1825-50

(HANCOCK SHAKER VILLAGE,
PITTSFIELD, MASSACHUSETTS)

A pair of religious or business leaders worked side by side.

April/May

30

4

1

5

2

6

3

Twin spiral stairs in
the Trustees' Office, 1839-41

(SHAKERTOWN AT PLEASANT HILL,
HARRODSBURG, KENTUCKY)

Sisters and Brethren
used separate stairs.

May

7

11

8

12

9

13

10

This morning we had the pleasure of sitting at the breakfast table with Eldress Antoinette & Sister Anna. It seemed much better to us than to be obliged to go away into a solitary little hall & eat and drink alone. To eat in solitude induces the blues & hurts digestion.

Elder Henry Blinn
May 14, 1873

Ministry Dining Room in the Center Family Dwelling, 1824-34

(SHAKERTOWN AT PLEASANT HILL, HARRODSBURG, KENTUCKY)

May

14

15

16

17

18

19

20

Henry Whiteman has finely [finally] cleared out, So much the better.

Sister Annie Williams
May 19, 1853

May

21

22

23

24

25

26

27

Brethren's Retiring Room,
Church Family Dwelling, 1830

(HANCOCK SHAKER VILLAGE,
PITTSFIELD, MASSACHUSETTS)

Four to five Brothers shared each room.
The Sisters' rooms were across the hall.

May/June

28

1

29

2

30

3

31

Patent model for chair
with tilting feet, 1852,
by George Donnell,
New Lebanon, New York

(PRIVATE COLLECTION)

The ball-and-socket feet
allowed the sitter to tip back
safely and without marring the floor.

June

4

5

6

7

8

9

10

We assemble this forenoon in meeting with hearts and souls devoted to God. It felt as if the windows of heaven were open and showers of blessings descended upon, yea, more than we had room to receive.

Sister Elizabeth Lovegrove
June 11, 1837

Meeting Room, Center Family Dwelling, 1824-34

(SHAKERTOWN AT PLEASANT HILL, HARRODSBURG, KENTUCKY)

June

11

12

13

14

15

16

17

A poor LOST SOUL — Charles D. Knight made the fatal choice to abscond from us. He was about 17 years of age, just entering the youthful stage of life. awful! awful!!! awful!!!!!!!!!!

Brother Elisha Blakeman
June 17, 1836

Stone walk

(HANCOCK SHAKER VILLAGE, PITTSFIELD, MASSACHUSETTS)

The path was wide enough for one, not two.

June

18

22

19

23

20

24

21

Waiting Room,
Church Family Dwelling, 1830

(HANCOCK SHAKER VILLAGE,
PITTSFIELD, MASSACHUSETTS)

THE SHAKER.

June/July

25

26

27

28

29

30

1

Round Stone Barn, 1826-64

(HANCOCK SHAKER VILLAGE,
PITTSFIELD, MASSACHUSETTS)

July

2

6

3

7

4

8

5

Table swift,
circa 1850-60

(HANCOCK SHAKER VILLAGE,
PITTSFIELD, MASSACHUSETTS)

A swift was useful for winding
a skein of yarn into a ball.
The cup on the top held the
ball during pauses in work.

July

9

10

11

12

13

14

15

Took all the boys and gave them a *ride out.* Go thro' Pittsfield & go on to *Lanseburgh Pond* where we stoped — hired 2 boats (one a sail boat the other a row boat) sailed & cruised about to our pleasure & had much recreation. Bathing also formed a beautiful & pleasant portion in our amusement. Eat our dinner drank soda, Lemon S. & C. Tartar took much pleasure, enjoyed a delightful scence & returned home.

Unidentified Brother July 12, 1845

Meetinghouse bench, circa 1825-50

(THE SHAKER MUSEUM AND LIBRARY, OLD CHATHAM, NEW YORK)

July

16

17

18

19

20

21

22

O Sorrow & joy Betsy Crossman, Mary Ann Mantle, Amy Reed have finished coloring blue wool, they began the 12th had 105 lb. & more than this had it all to wash over because Maria says we had such poor judgment & got the liquor too strong... & too hot I suppose. O Murder, every thing happens this awful year!!!!!!!

Sister Anna Dodgson
July 20, 1849

Sister's Shop and Diary, circa 1795-1820

(HANCOCK SHAKER VILLAGE, PITTSFIELD, MASSACHUSETTS)

Built-in storage, Church Family Dwelling, 1830

(HANCOCK SHAKER VILLAGE, PITTSFIELD, MASSACHUSETTS)

July

23

24

25

26

27

28

29

Eliza and I have attended union meeting in all the rooms in the house once or more in a place. The brethren and sisters set about 6 feet apart and those that are rather hard of hearing appear as well contented as any one that can hear all that is said.

Unidentified Shaker
July 27, 1839

July/August

30

31

1

2 Life is not reducible to £.s.d.

Life is not about a budget

3

4

5

This will I think be to me a long remembered day! My long loved companion Maria removes from me... We have spent ten years happily together without being disturbed by strife jar or contention & I really believe we have both felt more for each other's comfort than our own. Such a friend and companion as Maria is to me I never shall forget to all Eternity.

Sister Anna Dodgson
August 5, 1854

Tailoring Room

(HANCOCK SHAKER VILLAGE, PITTSFIELD, MASSACHUSETTS)

August

6

7

8

9

10

11

12

I began to make myself a new desk
for writing on:
And so it is while time does last,
I find enough to do,
With busy hands can't work so fast,
But what there's more to do.

Brother Henry DeWitt
August 1836

Lap desk, 1847, and revolving chair, circa 1860-70

(HANCOCK SHAKER VILLAGE, PITTSFIELD, MASSACHUSETTS)

August

13

15

14

16

17

19

18

Workbench, circa 1850

(THE FRUITLANDS MUSEUMS, HARVARD, MASSACHUSETTS)

August

20

24

21

25

22

26

23 James Shotko Lloyd

Francis Sears got the fire maker to wake him in the morning at ½ past 3, and he set out on a long journey, nobody knows where and nobody cares.

Sister Anna Dodgson
August 25, 1847

Spinning Wheel, New Lebanon, New York,
with oak rim, and ash wheel support

(HANCOCK SHAKER VILLAGE, PITTSFIELD, MASSACHUSETTS)

August / September

27

31

28

1

29

2

30

The Brethren go to mowing in the swamp. And Elder Ebenezer, Deacon Stephen, Elder Sister, Lydia, Electa and Samantha go and carry their dinner to them, which was: bread and butter, pye, strawberry sauce, fried potatoes, fresh meat, stewed beans and green tea sweetened with loaf sugar provided by the Ministry.

Brother John DeWitt
September 1, 1835

Dumbwaiter in the dining room, Church Family Dwelling, 1830

(HANCOCK SHAKER VILLAGE, PITTSFIELD, MASSACHUSETTS)

Dumbwaiters, or "sliding cupboards," carried food and dishes between the dining room and the kitchen below.

September

3

4

5

6

7

8

9

There has been a book read in the family that was put out by one Graham upon dieting and some of the family are trying to follow him in part, ie to eat bran bread clear potatoe tomatoes &c. and drink milk and water but not tea meat nor butter but Oh how their mouths water to see the fine beefsteak come on and to see the faithful eat of the good of the land.

Brother Aaron Bill
September 12, 1835

September

10

14

11

15

12

16

13

About 5 oclock P.M. we were invited to take a bath. This is one of the great luxuries we have been blest with since we left home. It is truly a blessing to be introduced to a bath of 10 inches deep and the vessel spacious enough to lie down your whole length. fed by a turn cock at the foot of the bath, and warm water enough to make it pleasant to the feel. O! it is too good to be rightly appreciated.

Eldress Nancy Moore
September 13, 1854

Water Tower, 1903
(THE UNITED SOCIETY OF SHAKERS, SABBATHDAY LAKE, MAINE)

September

17

21

18

22

19

23

20

Ministry Shop, circa 1873

(HANCOCK SHAKER VILLAGE, PITTSFIELD, MASSACHUSETTS)

Two Elders and two Eldresses served in the Ministry.

September

24

25

26

27

28

29

30

Pharmacy

(HANCOCK SHAKER VILLAGE, PITTSFIELD, MASSACHUSETTS)

The Shakers prepared medicines for home use and for sale from herbs and plants from their gardens or the woods.

October

1

5

2

6

3

7

4

Herb Shop in the Machine Shop
and Laundry, circa 1800

(HANCOCK SHAKER VILLAGE,
PITTSFIELD, MASSACHUSETTS)

October

8

12

9

13

10

14

11

The Sisters have been so very generous as to turn out & top the beets — They are worth many thanks. There are 500 bushels.

Brother Giles Avery
October 11, 1837

Detail of orchard and gardens
from map of Canterbury Shaker Village, New Hampshire, 1848, by Henry Blinn

(CANTERBURY SHAKER VILLAGE, INC., CANTERBURY, NEW HAMPSHIRE)

October

15

16

17

18

19

20

21

Lane in the Church Family

(THE UNITED SOCIETY OF SHAKERS,
SABBATHDAY LAKE, MAINE)

October

22

23 Philip John LLOYD

24

25

26

27

28

This morning I heard the sound of liberty!
Liberty from the bondage of old boots
and shoes, having spent 26 years
at the business.

Brother Henry DeWitt
October 30, 1852

October / November

29 Lawrence David McMaster

30

31

1

2

3

4

Boys' Shop, 1850,
and Spin House, 1816

(THE UNITED SOCIETY OF SHAKERS,
SABBATHDAY LAKE, MAINE)

November

5

9

6

10

7

11

8

While in our meeting, Novr. 9th, 1845, I saw a company of Angels descending, it appeared, from extreme heights in the west. — There were two companies, and they marched about 6 feet apart, twelve in a rank, and one hundred ranks. They carried between them a long vessel, having on each side a hundred handles, which was grasped by the first Angel of each rank: thus the vessel was carried along. Upon the top of the vessel burned a 100 lamps.

Sister Dorothy Ann Durgin November 9, 1845

A Present from the Natives Brought by One of Father Issachar's Tribe, 1848, by Polly Jane Reed, New Lebanon, New York

(THE WESTERN RESERVE HISTORICAL SOCIETY, CLEVELAND, OHIO)

Shaker "gift drawings" portrayed visions of the spirit world.

November

12

16

13

17

14

18

15

I'm now released from the boys
And from a deal of din and noise
And John is left to rule the roost
Without a second mate to boost
My Elders gave me a good name
So I do leave devoid of shame
Ha ha he he how glad I be
I've no more boys to trouble me.

Brother Elisha Blakeman November 20, 1844

November

19

23

20

24

21

25

22

Dining room doors and hall,
Church Family Dwelling, 1830

(HANCOCK SHAKER VILLAGE,
PITTSFIELD, MASSACHUSETTS)

Brethren and Sisters
entered by separate doors.

November / December

26

27

28

29

30

1

2

Harness maker's vise, 1835

(THE SHAKER MUSEUM AND LIBRARY, OLD CHATHAM, NEW YORK)

December

3

4

5

6

7

8

9

Evening at the Center Family

(SHAKERTOWN AT PLEASANT HILL
HARRODSBURG, KENTUCKY)

December

10

11

12

13

14

15

16

As I was riding on my sleigh,
Upon the mountain high;
A zero cold and windy day,
Did cause the snow to fly.
I wished myself within the shop,
Where I could warm my toes;
And apples eat all roasted hot
Which pleasant summer grows.

Brother Elisha Blakeman
December 1837

Sleighriding past the Round Stone Barn, 1826,
and Poultry House, 1876

(HANCOCK SHAKER VILLAGE, PITTSFIELD, MASSACHUSETTS)

December

17

21

18

22

19

23

20

Some people think it is vulgar to laugh, but let such stand in life's gloomy shadows if they choose. As a *general* rule the best men and women laugh the most. Good, round, hearty, side-shaking laughter is health for everybody, for the dyspeptic it is life.

Brother Calvin Fairchild
December 24, 1868

Christmas Hymn.

Long this day our song shall honor,
c d c a f f d e f
'Tis a day of holy things,
g a g e c c d e
Zion's God hath look'd upon her,
f e d e f
g a g e g g
Heaven with songs of triumph rings.
g f e d c g a b c
Praise and glory in the highest,
g a g e c a c c a g f
Saints and angels now proclaim
e f g g e c c d e
Thou that ne'er our prayer deny-est
f f d e f
e e f g e g
We will praise thy holy name.
g a g e c g a b c

We will run the race before us,
We will walk the heavenly road,
Till we join the angelic chorus,
In the mansion of our God.
O, our Father bless the nations
Let them now return to thee,

December

24

25

26

27

28

29

30

31

Christmastime in the Church Family Dwelling, 1830

(HANCOCK SHAKER VILLAGE, PITTSFIELD, MASSACHUSETTS)

The bell rope went from the roof to the kitchen
six floors below to save steps.

Photo credits:
The photographs are shown opposite
the following dates:

Michael Freeman

January 1, 8, 15, 22. February 5, 26.
March 5, 12, 26. April 2, 16, 23, 30. May 7, 14, 21.
July 23, 29. August 9, 13, 27. September 10, 24.
October 15, 29. November 19. Dec 3.

Paul Rocheleau

Page 5. January 29. February 12, 19. March 19. April 9.
May 28. June 4, 11, 18, 25. July 2, 9, 16, 30.
August 20. September 17. October 1, 8.
November 5, 26. December 10, 17, 24.

previous page

Christmas Hymn
HANCOCK SHAKER VILLAGE